Bob Alves and Don Ro...

THE NOT-FOR-PROFIT

CEO's

GUIDE TO IMPROVING
ORGANIZATIONAL PERFORMANCE

HOW TO MAKE SURE YOUR BUSINESS STRATEGY
DRIVES YOUR TECHNOLOGY INVESTMENTS

First Printing, 2015

ISBN: 978-1-329-14787-4

TABLE OF CONTENTS

From the Authors

As you know massive change has occurred in the way not-for-profits like yours communicate with donors. Here's an example of how fast this change is occurring: Just look at the photos below showing the difference between the groups of people who showed up at the Vatican in 2005 to welcome Pope Benedict compared to those who welcomed Pope Francis in 2013.[1] Nearly everyone in the entire crowd in the newer photo is using a mobile device.

More than likely, the systems you bought just a few years ago — and still use today to manage your donor data — were not designed and conceived to take full advantage of the Internet. And, they are probably now just about obsolete because they cannot adequately handle your needs in a changing and fast-moving world.

If you are considering making technology investments anytime in the next three years, Advanced Solutions International (ASI) can help you now. The two of us founded ASI in 1991 and have grown it to the largest, founder-owned software company in the world for donor- and member-based not-for-profits.

---

[1] 2005 photo: AP Photo/Luca Bruno; 2013 photo: AP Photo/Michael Sohn.

We wrote this book specifically with C-level leaders in mind. So, please don't delegate looking at it to your department managers. This conversation is simply too important and too high-level. It centers on topics your department managers are not comfortable discussing and ones that, frankly, need your leadership to make the tough decisions that will successfully navigate your organization into the future. You'll want to be sure to take full advantage of what we have to offer. This book is based on our work since 1991 with more than 4,000 not-for-profits in more than 25 countries.

We believe we have found important answers to the questions you should be asking about how to position your not-for-profit for the future. We have found our most successful clients make sure their business strategy drives their technology investments. These clients learn about themselves continuously from their operational activities. As a result, they use this knowledge to continuously improve their organizations' performance.

To help clients move forward as quickly and confidently as possible, ASI created a special program called the "Success Partnership Program" (SPP) that identifies your most pressing problems, helps you get organized, saves you time and money, lowers your risk of investing in the wrong technology assets, and keeps you from being disappointed once again because you did not achieve the expected return on your investment. This *"Performance Improvement Preview"* is just one of the valuable resources we offer and we'll discuss in the following pages.

The leaders of our client organizations see us as a trusted advisor for their strategic investments in technology.

We offer a unique approach to help you align your strategy and operations so that your future investments result in long-term, continuous performance improvement — instead of needing to start over every five to seven years. More than 750 clients have been with us for 15 years or more; they're accruing major benefits from their technology investments because they are getting great results year after year.

In the following pages we don't just talk theory. We provide the hands-on tools you need — proven best practice strategies, solutions to problems, self-assessments, and results-based case studies from real clients to help you gain insight into what you must do if you want to adapt to the massive changes upon us. Our intention is to "lift the veil" and share behind-the-scenes insights that can show you how to avoid modern-day software selection and implementation pitfalls while aligning your strategy and technology to create a lasting advantage for your organization. Most importantly, we show you how to achieve continuous performance improvement for your organization.

We offer you this book as a practical resource. Use it wisely and the rewards will be great!

Wishing you great success,

Bob Alves
Chairman and CEO
Advanced Solutions International (ASI)

Don Robertson
President and CTO

Chapter 1 — Making Yourself the Leader of Your Technology Investments

Like most not-for-profit executives today, you're no doubt looking for the best ways to successfully lead your organization into the future. But, how on earth do you do this when technology is changing so quickly, the economy is still sluggish, and your donors' needs are constantly growing and becoming more sophisticated?

In his book, *Race for Relevance*, Harrison Coerver talks about the need for leaders of not- for-profits to approach technology investments in a new and different way. He goes on to say:

> ***"The adoption and exploitation of technology, particularly information and communication technologies must become an integral component of the organization's functioning and performance."***[2]

But to make this happen, senior leadership needs to be directly engaged. Mr. Coerver makes these and other great points that we will continue to drive home throughout our book.

---

[2] Harrison Coerver and Mary Byers, Race for Relevance (Washington, DC: ASAE) Kindle edition.

In working with more than 4,000 clients since 1991, Advanced Solutions International (ASI), has become the largest, founder-owned software company in the world for not-for-profits and associations. Through this work, we've earned our position as a trusted advisor to the executives of these organizations and have learned the most successful best-practice lessons first-hand.

We're going to share the behind-the-scenes tips and strategies you'll need to:

- Increase donor engagement/retention
- Reduce costs, and
- Improve overall organizational performance

Using Best Practices to Lead Your Team

Over the years, we've learned a lot from our clients and they've learned a lot from us as well. The most successful not-for-profit CEOs adhere to the following four best practices that stand out from all the rest:

1) **Let the business strategy drive technology decision making**. With a clear business strategy you can design your operational systems and activities to achieve your goals. This is the basis for an environment of continuous performance improvement.
2) **Focus on becoming a "continuous learning organization."** You must learn from your operational activities all the time, at every step of the way, to realize continuous performance improvement.

3) **Ensure your data is accurate, up-to-date and easily accessible.** Clean, real-time data that can be reported on and analyzed is crucial to continuous performance improvement — you can never underestimate its importance.

4) **Recognize that your website is your business system and vice versa.** You can no longer separate the two —a website providing personalized, dynamic content based on your donor data, is your future engine for engagement and retention.

Top 4 Not-for-Profit Best Practices

1) *Let your business strategy drive technology decision making.*

2) *Focus on becoming a "continuous learning organization."*

3) *Ensure your data is accurate, up-to-date, and easily accessible.*

4) *Recognize that your website is your business system and vice versa.*

Examining Your Existing Tools to Enable Continuous Performance Improvement

Our vision for success as your trusted advisor is to help you see that an Engagement Management System (EMS) is a critical management tool — not "just software." We want to help you enable continuous performance improvement in your organization by using EMS tools to help you constantly learn from your business activities and ultimately reach your goals. Adopting the Engagement Management System mindset allows our clients to embrace the growing importance of their donors as key users of their systems, whether from a mobile device or traditional PC.

We also want to help you understand the importance of learning from these transactions. To do this successfully, all donor activities need to be collected in a single database and all data needs to be easily accessible for analysis. Your EMS must work the way the world works today so you can capture this data in real time.

We all know the last few years have brought massive change to the communication and information technologies we use. Consequently, your donors are changing how they communicate with you — and faster than you think. Therefore, your donor management system needs to be able to adapt to and support these changes. Private communities, social engagement, on-line commerce, on-line donations, etc. must be part of your Engagement Management System. This means you need to embrace the idea that your business system is your website and vice versa.

To adapt to the massive changes happening, you must be willing to fuse your database and your website into one easy-to-use application. Your website needs to allow donors convenient self-service options so that they can do whatever they need and want to do from anywhere they want, at any time they want, and from any device they choose.

> *Your website needs to allow donors convenient self-service options so that they can do whatever they need and want to do from anywhere they want, at any time they want, and from any device they choose.*

ASI's own *2015 Global Benchmark Report on Fundraising Performance* surveyed hundreds of not-for-profit executives and found that 29% generated up to half of all their donations online. And, the M+R 2014 Benchmark Study[3] found that online giving increased 14% from the prior year.

This means you need to be ready. It's vital that your business system/website offers the flexibility you'll need to make necessary changes on-the-fly to ensure donors have the options they need to make their lives easier and keep them engaged with your organization.

---

[3] *M+R 2014 Benchmark Study,* http://mrbenchmarks.com/, **Page 26**

> *29% of not-for-profit executives generated up to half of all their donations online.*

When we work with new clients, many are surprised that we talk about helping them make the best decisions all the way through the selection/implementation process. We do this to ensure they're able to improve their organizations' performance.

> *We don't have sales executives, we have "Performance Improvement Specialists" specifically for fundraising organizations who bring that unique perspective and focus to every meeting they have with clients.*

This book provides a blueprint to help you achieve the following:

1) Choose a donor management system that can effectively support your organization as technology continues to change.
2) Increase your donor engagement/retention and, as a result, continuously improve your performance. This results in excess resources you can reinvest in your not-for-profit year after year.

3) Conduct a *"Performance Improvement Preview"* of a modern system before you make a technology investment.

Practical Options for Leading Your Team to Smart Technology Investments

Another unique advantage ASI offers is our "Success Partnership Program." This includes a *"Performance Improvement Preview"* that lets potential clients see our iMIS 20 Engagement Management System (EMS) in a real-world environment using their own data and processes. We make this innovative program available to not-for-profit executives like you because we're confident that it will show you precisely how you can benefit from our expertise as trusted advisors to thousands of organizations worldwide.

> *The Success Partnership Program (SPP) includes a "Performance Improvement Preview" that lets potential clients experience our iMIS 20 Engagement Management System.*

Many of your peers have already taken advantage of this program and you should, too. There's no risk — the low-cost engagement fee can be applied to your new system if you decide iMIS 20 is right for you, but either way you come away with a personalized requirements document you can use to make a highly informed decision about your future technology investments no matter what you decide to invest in or who you work with.

How to Use this Book

We cite a lot of data in this book. Our primary research is internal — based on our experience with 4,000 not-for-profits and associations worldwide. We gather many success stories and best practices from the field — working with clients like you. We have also conducted a global survey of fundraising executives and published it in our 2015 Global Benchmark Report on Fundraising Performance (see the addendum for an executive summary of the report.)

Our secondary research comes from formal studies, such as studies from the TCC research group and other sources, all of which focus on the not-for-profit space.

This book is divided into three major sections:

- An outline of the challenges that not-for-profits are currently facing — some of which you may recognize and a few that you perhaps weren't even aware of.
- An overview of the new Engagement Management System (EMS) that can tackle the challenges of today and tomorrow.
- A summary of the results you can expect to achieve with an EMS.

We've also included lots of tips, self-assessment exercises, and success stories you can learn from. We invite you to take full advantage of the advice we've gathered to propel your not-for-profit forward.

Chapter 2 — Assessing Your Current Situation

Before you dive into the tips, strategies, and best practices we've loaded into this book, it's important to stop and take stock of your organization.

> *... the behavior that distinguishes the quality management team is the execution of tactics and tasks that propel the organization toward achieving its stated mission and strategy.*

Often times, when working with senior executives, strategy has an independent life of its own. Senior management teams love to strategize and boldly proclaim their mission and donor-service commitments on their websites. The public communication of strategy appeals to those who want to separate themselves from the day-to-day tedium of managing a successful not-for-profit. But the behavior that distinguishes the quality management teams is execution of tactics and tasks that propel the not-for-profit toward its stated mission and strategy. In our experience this is harder to find than one might think. Strategy is important but strategy without execution is worthless.

The world is full of great ideas and even internally and externally sponsored studies on what you should do to increase the impact of your not-for-profit. But, prior to exploring the successful action steps you should implement, we ask that you take the 25-point Success Assessment below. This will help set a benchmark for where your organization is today compared to where it should be.

25-Point Fundraising Success Assessment

This Fundraising Success Assessment breaks down the four areas that contribute to not-for-profit success—***Recruit, Engage, Measure, and Grow***.

Each individual section is strategically important to your business success and links to a collective approach that will help you reach your mission objectives and profitability goals. Indicators of success in one section but failure in another will help you and your team identify operational gaps hindering maximum organizational performance.

By evaluating your group's ability to implement and sustain an integrated revenue capture program, our process can help you take steps not just to survive but to thrive. All information collected is confidential.

The questions probe strategic and tactical issues on how your organization operates. Is this the end analysis of your organization's ability to grow revenue? No, of course not. But the Fundraising Success Assessment does help you identify specific gaps in your organization's best practices approach and peak performance capabilities.

Check the box that most accurately applies to your fundraising organization. If the question does not apply, skip it. If you can't answer the question but it does apply to your current business model, seek the appropriate department head and ask for an answer. If you can't get a clear answer, select "No."

Recruit:

How do you win new business? Recruit new donors and retain existing ones with integrated, multi-channel marketing campaigns.

1. Do you have a written and automated strategic plan to acquire donors in underserved groups within your prospect base?

   ☐ Yes   ☐ No

2. Do you and your executive team regularly review reports that track the number of donor service calls that are not completed (or not responded to) the same day and then carried over to the next day?

   ☐ Yes   ☐ No

3. Do you have a written and automated process designed to welcome, thank and retain new donors more effectively so that they feel that participating in your organization is a good use of their time and money?

   ☐ Yes   ☐ No

4. Does your information system provide reports or other ways to analyze what your new and current donors expect from your organization so that you can effectively tailor marketing and service messages in your communications?

    ☐ Yes   ☐ No

5. Does your donor development team have sufficient time each week to identify and speak with prospective donors personally?

    ☐ Yes   ☐ No

Engage:

Empower donors to engage with your organization and with other donors – anytime, anywhere.

6. Do you have a consistent written and automated process for sustaining donor engagement at a high level so that you have a large pool of future volunteer leaders?

    ☐ Yes   ☐ No

7. Do you have a written and implemented method for simplifying, standardizing and automating business processes to manage business operations that you execute annually more efficiently?

☐ Yes   ☐ No

8. Can you monitor whether each staff member is following the agreed upon business rules and practices for using information systems that set by your leadership team so that you can rely on the data in the system when making strategic decisions?

☐ Yes   ☐ No

9. Do you have a written and implemented process to train new employees on fundamental processes and tasks within your organization so that they can become immediately productive?

☐ Yes   ☐ No

10. Are at least 90% of donor email addresses, mailing addresses, and phone numbers on file confirmed, current and accurate so that you can communicate effectively with each of your donor groups instantly?

☐ Yes   ☐ No

11. Do you have written and automated procedures in place that are implemented by your staff to satisfactorily address supporter service issues?

☐ Yes ☐ No

12. Do you regularly measure how happy and satisfied your donors are with the website, services you offer, and operations of the organization, so you can share that information with staff to tailor future services and develop new programs?

☐ Yes ☐ No

Measure:

Continually measure and improve marketing campaigns and donor engagement efforts.

13. Do you have written and implemented policies and procedures to address Payment Card Industry Data Security Standards (PCI-DSS) from all credit card (via web, telephone, mail or in person) transactions related to your organization?

☐ Yes ☐ No

14. Can you measure what each donor means to your organization in financial terms?

☐ Yes ☐ No

15. Do you calculate projected cash flow operational needs 3 to 5 years out?

☐ Yes ☐ No

16. Are you able to integrate your accounting system with other information systems, such as your donor management, event registration, order processing, and online commerce systems — without customization?

☐ Yes ☐ No

17. Can the executive leadership and staff easily access the information you collect about a donor on their own, from one source (with no information maintained in extraneous / redundant data sources such as Excel spreadsheets, rolodexes and the like) to obtain a complete picture of each donor's engagement during his or her involvement with the organization?

☐ Yes ☐ No

18. Today, do you have real time information proactively available to help you manage strategic, technical, operational and financial needs as they develop?

☐ Yes ☐ No

Grow:

Increase new donor acquisition, improve donor retention, and identify new opportunities

19. Various barriers such as organizational silos, inadequate staff training, custom programming, and inadequate financial reserves can inhibit your ability to respond quickly to challenges and opportunities. Are you able to roll out emergency initiatives within a week and major new programs within 60 days?

☐ Yes   ☐ No

20. Maintaining multiple, diverse revenue sources often requires a separate business structure and processes for each. Do you have an effective structure, business processes and trained staff to attract, develop and maintain new sources of revenue?

☐ Yes   ☐ No

21. Over the last five years, have you averaged consistent donor retention of 35% or more?

☐ Yes   ☐ No

22. Over the last five years, have you averaged consistent growth of at least 10% per year in donors and revenue?

☐ Yes   ☐ No

23. Does your organization have a written, long-range strategic plan approved by the Board and currently implemented?

☐ Yes   ☐ No

24. Does your annual budget provide a written blueprint, reviewed quarterly, that directs your staff on action steps they need to take to achieve your organizational goals for that year and beyond?

☐ Yes   ☐ No

25. Are you 100% confident that if either your physical offices became uninhabitable or you lost your key technical staff, it would not cause any downtime for your website and donor systems?

☐ Yes   ☐ No

Results:

Give yourself 4% for each "yes" answer. The test is not a complete assessment of your revenue growth and performance improvement potential, but is a snapshot of where you may be versus where you need to be.

60% and below

Creating efficiencies to enable your organization to effectively grow each year (even in down markets) will be difficult as your current business success model cannot achieve year-over-year sustainable growth. If your revenues are increasing, it is an anomaly, not a methodology or a business process, and has specific financial and operational leakage issues and corporate instability exposure. To fix this position, you need to redesign your business and the integration of your operations, fundraising and strategy processes into one donor needs-driven approach.

61% to 80%

Your current business-growth model has some of the best practice attributes needed to grow not-for-profit revenue year-over-year using a planned process. Some of your business structure may need to be adjusted to maximize long-term organizational growth goals.

80% and above

Your not-for-profit structure maximizes organizational growth capabilities and uses an inter-department alignment that focuses on strategy linked to action steps. You have built a sustainable pattern that should foster continued success for you and your team.

Chapter 3 — The Challenge: Improving Engagement and Organizational Performance

Our internal research — from working with more than 4,000 not-for-profits and not-for-profits around the world — shows that the top two problems for fundraising organizations are: 1) increasing engagement and 2) improving organizational performance.

Engagement involves:

- Donor Retention and Acquisition
- Donor Satisfaction
- Employee Satisfaction
- Data Integrity
- Brand Enhancement

Improving performance means:

- Reaching Your Goals
- Maximizing Staff and Volunteer Productivity
- Managing Risk
- Controlling Operating Costs
- Keeping up with Changing Technology

Understanding the History of DMS/CRM Systems

Donor Management Software (DMS) and Constituent Relationship Management (CRM) software were initially designed for staff that needed to perform administrative tasks, such as processing donations and registrations for events. As time went on, organizations decided to add donor websites, such as portals and social communities. These supported better engagement of donors, but each was still a separate system, with separate projects and separate budgets. Then, of course, you had to deal with taking financial transactions from these donors.

Later, the need arose to connect the not-for-profit's website with donor databases. Most of the time, each of these add-ons to the DMS or CRM system had its own name and address database. And that had to be connected to the main database by programmers doing expensive and time-consuming integration projects.

Today nearly everyone is using mobile devices to get and give information — and your donors want to be able to do that through your website. This may force the creation of yet another specialized name and address database if you're using a traditional system. All of these databases become silos of information that are not designed to work together. This causes ongoing complexity, which leads to more problems. Supporting different technologies and complex integrations becomes a stumbling block to upgrades.

The total cost of ownership of a traditional DMS/CRM system with these add-ons is skyrocketing. The cost to purchase and maintain products from multiple vendors — as well as the services to support them — is unacceptable. And that doesn't even account for management time. Here's the scary thing: many not-for-profits are unaware that they have a choice and don't need to buy this dysfunctional, antiquated model ever again. There is a better, more modern approach that will increase engagement, control costs, and deliver continuous performance improvement.

The diagram below illustrates the many problems of traditional systems:

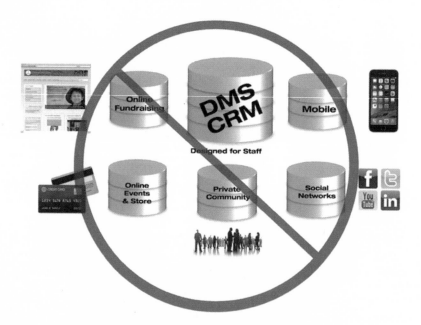

- *Complex Integrations*
- *Disparate Products & Vendors*
- *Higher Cost of Ownership*

Evaluating Your True Ability to Measure Performance

It might surprise you to know that the traditional systems readily available today are not the best way to meet the challenges of tomorrow. But, no doubt you're already experiencing that first hand. Our findings show that the traditional system that most organizations use today — such as a DMS or CRM system positioned as "state-of-the-art" —cannot deliver continuous performance improvement.

What Does it Cost?

The traditional approach typically involves multiple systems (to manage donor data, websites, mobile, social, etc.) To work together, these systems need to be customized — and this customization needs to be maintained on an ongoing basis by vendors who are essentially incented to keep the system as complicated as possible. This trickles down and causes your staff costs to rise to further support all of the system complexity.

Are Your Management Tools Effective?

Our research shows traditional systems are ineffective management tools. They destroy opportunities for continuous performance improvement because they are often built on disparate databases. This creates roadblocks to any kind of disciplined data management, disconnects operational activities from strategic goals, and leads to unreliable management reporting.

> *A recent analysis of nearly 2,500 not-for-profits by consulting firm TCC Group has found that those exhibiting multiple 'R&D behaviors," such as gathering data directly from program recipients to determine how to improve programs and evaluating programs to figure out what works rather than deciding if it works, grow revenues more than twice as fast as those not-for-profits exhibiting no such behaviors, even after controlling for other factors.[4]*

But, if your system isn't capable of gathering, analyzing, and then implementing this intelligence, you could be left in the underperforming group.

What Opportunities Are You Losing?

> *...we estimate that the average not-for-profit with a traditional system loses a minimum of 10-15% of potential revenue per year due to poor management decisions based on flawed data.*

There is also the problem of high opportunity costs or lost opportunity because traditional systems are ineffective in growing and maintaining donor engagement.

---

[4] Peter York, TCC Group Briefing Paper: *Success by Design,* Web, Retrieved January 28, 2015, http://www.tccgrp.com/pdfs/7-21_TCC_Briefing_Paper_LR.pdf, *page 5.*

Traditional systems are not suited for the way the world works today — they were built for a time in the past. Not-for-profits now need to provide donors with convenient, flexible web interfaces that make it easy to engage. They need to provide information exactly how the donors want it, when they want it, and from wherever they want it.

There are several reasons the old approach fails, but we estimate that the average not-for-profit with a traditional system loses a minimum of 10-15% of potential revenue per year due to poor management decisions based on flawed data. Or, in instances when management can't make a decision because it has no data. And that opportunity cost only grows when figuring in lost donor engagement and retention, not to mention the significantly reduced lifetime value.

Since August 2013, a group of organizations (Robert Frances Group, Chaordix Inc., Principal Consulting LLC, and the IBM Information Governance Community) surveyed, interviewed and analyzed data collected from 600 business and IT professionals.[5]

Their results showed that 66% of respondents knew about customer-related problems that stem from poor data quality and 73% acknowledged that poor data caused them to lose some or all of a client's business. While these findings were most prevalent in companies with more than 10,000 employees, they were true for all other size ranges as well. And the lessons of these commercial enterprises are just as relevant for not-for-profits.

---

[5] *Enterprise Executive*, "Poor Data Quality Costs More Than You Think," Cal Braunstein and Stuart Selip, November/December 2014, Pages 52-59.

Of the 326 not-for-profit executives responding to a survey for ASI's 2015 Global Benchmark Report on Fundraising Performance, 45% reported they have seen retention rates decline or remain stagnant in the past year.

Examining Your Return on Investment (ROI) from Technology

The chart below shows what it might look like over a seven-year period if you invest in a traditional system. Basically, you're going to see weak net revenue gains and weak net revenue contributions. This graph shows that you might grow revenue somewhat from Year 1 to Year 7, but you're also going to see your costs go up. And if revenue and costs go up at the same rate, you're not realizing continuous improvement.

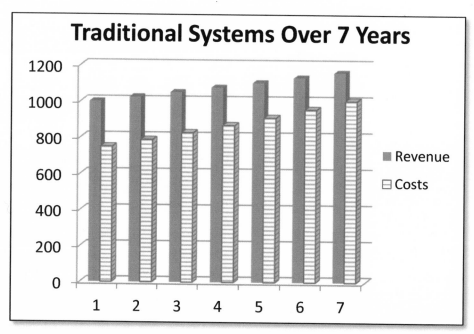

Source: Internal ASI research/client feedback.

Determining What's Driving Up Your Costs

If you select a system today by going to a trade show, hiring a system selection consultant, or relying on conventional wisdom, there's a high probability you'll buy a traditional system with disparate solutions cobbled together to meet your needs. This will result in higher costs from multiple applications and vendors, duplication/overlap, and custom services required to support and integrate the various applications to help you address donor engagement.

> *Feedback from our clients about their past experiences shows that services account for more than 60% of DMS and CRM system expenses.*

This antiquated traditional model will also greatly increase the amount of internal staff and volunteer time that goes into managing the old approach. Feedback from our clients about their past experiences shows that services account for more than 60% of DMS and CRM system expenses. The majority of these costs go toward systems integration, customizations, difficult upgrades, and software bug fixes over time.

Assessing Real Costs of Your Technology

You'll see in the chart below that traditional DMS and CRM systems cost a lot more than you think to maximize donor engagement over time. The legend on the right shows all the things you actually need to do to offer the top-class service your donors need. So, you may start out with a certain new system budget in Year 1 but by the time you add in all the upgrades, customizations, integrations, etc., those costs could triple by Year 3.

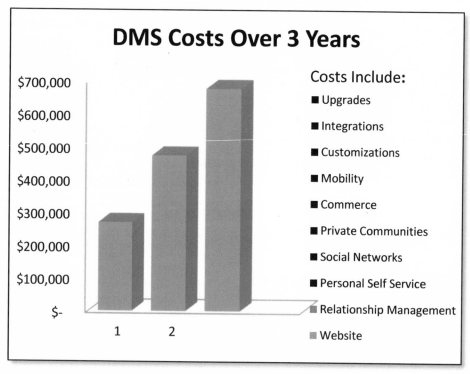

Source: Internal ASI research/client feedback.

Does this surprise you? Well it doesn't end there. There are also hidden costs. Managers and staff have to look after all of these extra elements. They have to manage data silos and they have multiple vendors to deal with. These multiple systems have multiple integration points. That carries overhead. Then there's customization and training. All of this is costly and impacts your management and related staff time.

Assessing Management and Staff Costs of Your Technology

In the three-year timeframe we've discussed, you may see the burden on your staff escalate significantly. You may have to add two staff and deal with the impact on the existing staff to handle the system. So, we're going to add another $360,000 to the first 3 years to account for the staff time in the chart below.

Source: Internal ASI research/client feedback.

Apply Simple Math to All Costs to Get a Real Number

When we add the management impact of these systems into the equation, the costs grow even larger. In this next chart, you can see how a system initially started at $225,000, but the actual cost is $1,037,500 by Year 3 — about 5 times the original cost, when you include the impact on staff. So, no matter what your starting point is, you can expect to spend 400% more with a traditional DMS or CRM system when you factor in the impact of staffing and service costs.

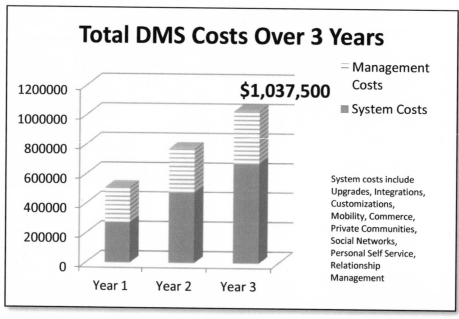

Source: Internal ASI research/client feedback.

Chapter 4 — The Solution: Understanding a Modern Engagement Management System (EMS)

Evaluating Your Management Style

Everyone agrees that massive change is upon us, especially in the areas of information, communications, and the technologies we use for these. Historically, this type of massive change has been a great opportunity for innovation and even re-invention of organizations like yours. However, in 2015 there are powerful vested interests in preserving the status quo. There is a high probability — if you leave technology decisions to your staff or conventional methods — your organization will invest in the wrong technology platform. As with any major change in direction, the mandate must come from the top. The CEO needs to lead the transition.

> *There is a high probability — if you leave technology decisions to your staff or conventional methods — your organization will invest in the wrong technology platform. As with any major change in direction, the mandate must come from the top. The CEO needs to lead the transition.*

In *Race for* Relevance, one of the most popular not-for-profit management books of the past decade, author Harrison Coerver talks about the need for leaders of not- for-profits to approach technology investments in a new and different way. He goes on to say:

> *"The adoption and exploitation of technology, particularly information and communication technologies, must become an integral component of the organization's functioning and performance."[6]*

But to make this happen, senior leadership needs to be directly engaged. Your leadership in making technology decisions could have a pivotal impact on your organization's future success. No one else can bring the strategic perspective into the thinking process.

---

[6] Harrison Coerver and Mary Byers, Race for Relevance (Washington, DC: ASAE) Kindle edition.

You need to let your people know it is okay to think out-of-the-box and let these forward thinking ideas compete with the more traditional ideas. After all, the world has drastically changed.

4 Best Practices That Will Ensure Your Success

In our work with thousands of clients worldwide over the past 20+ years, we've heard a common theme from the most successful organizations — those that have withstood economic pressures, evolving technologies, and demographic changes. They all subscribe to the following four key best practices:

1) **Let the business strategy drive technology decision making.** With a clear business strategy you can design your operational systems and activities to help you achieve your goals. This is the basis for an environment of continuous performance improvement.

2) **Focus on becoming a "continuous learning organization."** You must learn from your operational activities all the time, at every step of the way, to achieve continuous performance improvement.

3) **Ensure your data is accurate, up-to-date and easily accessible.** Clean, real-time data that can be reported on and analyzed is crucial to continuous performance improvement — you can never underestimate its importance.

4) **Recognize that your website is your business system and vice versa.** You can no longer separate the two —a website that provides your donors with personalized, dynamic content based on your organization's constituent data is absolutely critical to engagement and retention.

Our research shows that clients can achieve significant gains from a single, modern system specifically designed for the way not-for-profits actually work today.

> *The greatest gains come from clients who focus on driving continuous performance improvement through best practices. These clients focus on maximizing donor engagement, particularly web-based engagement.*

To do this, it's a must that you build your new system on a single database and consolidate as many applications as possible to reduce cost and complexity. This includes fusing all donor-oriented websites with your donor database to create an all-inclusive system. But some things are easy to say and hard to do.

When selecting a new system you want to minimize customization, and invest in a solution that allows you to meet most of your needs right out-of-the-box. You also need the flexibility to tailor the system without unknowingly creating complexities that will block your upgrade path and drive up future costs with ongoing customization. You want to be very careful about adding third-party solutions to the system; it's best to use only authorized third-party products that allow you to maintain your upgrade path. This may limit your choices but it is critical to the creation of an efficient, upgradeable software platform with easily accessible data.

These best practice strategies enable you to use your system as a management tool, reduce data integration needs (and the related costs), improve donor engagement, and drive continuous performance improvement. What not-for-profit doesn't want that?

What Forward Thinking Leaders are Expecting from Their Technology Investments

We've reviewed traditional system challenges and successful decision-making strategies and now it's time to look at alternatives to help solve your most pressing concerns.

WHAT IF … there was a better system?

What if this system was a much better management tool because it could enable continuous performance improvement? A system that was built for the way the world works today would be more effective at driving and expanding engagement.

WHAT IF … a new system could increase revenues while controlling expenses?

What if the system was a much better value because — instead of exploding costs — it actually drove down the on-going expense and complexity of your technology platform? Revenues would go up, costs would go down, and the delta would be a major contribution to your performance. Isn't that what every not-for-profit needs?

The chart below illustrates the growing revenue and flattening costs over 7 years of a modern engagement management system.

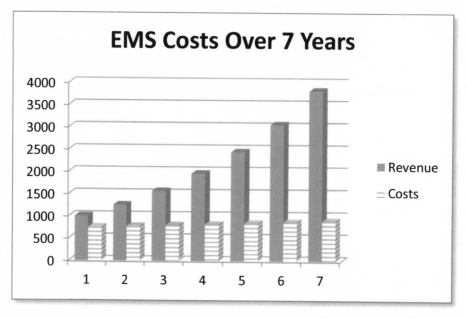

Source: Internal ASI research/client feedback.

WHAT IF ... all of this was in one system?

What if you had a single system that maximized your donor engagement and retention, while increasing staff/volunteer productivity and lowering costs? A traditional DMS system drives up costs due to the duplication of applications required to try to improve donor engagement. In the chart below, the applications and services required to support those applications are listed on the right. Based on feedback from clients who previously used DMS systems, we estimate that services accounted for more than 60% of their costs (for integration, customization, difficult upgrades and bug fixes over time.) If you could do all of this in just one system, the majority of the services required would be eliminated and management time would be reduced.

The bottom line is that one system would be much less expensive to operate and would yield better results.

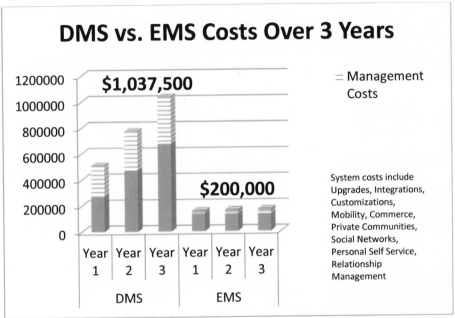

DMS vs. EMS Costs Over 3 Years

Source: Internal ASI research/client feedback.

WHAT IF … you could reduce your costs by 80%?

What if a modern engagement management system could be implemented for the actual price quoted in the first year — so all you're paying are small maintenance fees going forward? If you implement an engagement management system in the first year using out-of-the-box solutions for the items listed in the chart above, you could reduce your costs by 80%. Even if you tailored the system somewhat, you could still create a dramatic savings over the traditional DMS model.

No need to wonder "What if" any longer; the future is here and it's called an "Engagement Management System" (EMS). Let us show you how we do this.

iMIS 20 Engagement Management System (EMS)™

With the iMIS 20 Engagement Management System (EMS)™, we are able to offer our clients a major business advantage. The vision for this web-based engagement model is: "Your donors can get whatever they need from you via your website and you have a record of it."

iMIS 20 is a full-cycle EMS designed to engage your donors, staff and volunteers anytime, anywhere, and on any device. It's one system, one database that includes:

- Donor management
- Self-service
- Online donations
- Social engagement
- Private communities
- Mobile access
- Donor websites

And, it's all in a single, seamless cloud-based system.

iMIS 20 greatly reduces data integration needs and complexities while improving donor intelligence and driving continuous performance improvement.

Only iMIS 20 provides nearly unlimited flexibility while you stay on the upgrade path (by avoiding expensive custom programming that will raise your long-term costs.)

The system empowers you to easily create and personalize donor self-service, community, and mobile web pages without any programming. By implementing a complete, highly professional engagement management system with thousands of useful features right out-of-the-box, you can extend the functionality of the system without blocking the upgrade path.

Only iMIS 20 eliminates costly integration efforts, gathers better donor intelligence for donor engagement, and helps you make smarter business decisions. iMIS 20 is built on the RiSE web engagement platform that has the flexibility to work with your existing Content Management System (CMS) or — for many organizations — the power to manage your entire web presence.

Benefits of an EMS

There are many benefits for an organization to move from the old DMS approach to an EMS today. The primary reason is that you need to be ready for the future. An Engagement Management System will address most of the modern challenges facing you today; a DMS simply will not. The iMIS 20 EMS was designed for the way your donors work today — built on a web engagement platform that will help you make smarter business decisions.

iMIS 20 can help you increase revenues, grow your donor base and reduce costs. You will also lower your risk by working with a quality supplier who has been ranked #1 in client satisfaction. More importantly, our approach will help you become a learning organization, which will deliver and enable a continuous performance improvement culture that will help you improve your operations consistently year after year after year.

The era of traditional DMS and CRM systems is over because they were never designed to support the way your not-for-profit works today or how it will operate in the future.

You need the iMIS 20 EMS that will allow your donors to register for events from their mobile phones after a workout, contribute to your fundraising campaigns while waiting for a flight, or connect with others who share their passion for your cause in one of your private communities. You also need an all-inclusive system that makes your staff and volunteers more productive and communication easier. With iMIS 20, you'll have one system that engages everyone.

Unique Advantages of Working with Us

iMIS 20 delivers three distinct advantages over alternative systems:

1) By focusing on recruiting, engaging, measuring, and growing, we help your not-for-profit achieve continuous performance improvement.
2) You can offer your donors access to your system for everything they may need — anytime, from wherever they are, from any device. That's our Engagement Management model.
3) RiSE, our powerful web development platform, allows you to fuse your business system, donor-oriented websites and traditional fundraising applications into one system. This powerful capability allows you to provide donors with easy, flexible web interfaces, thereby allowing engagement with your donors to sky rocket.

Chapter 5 – The Results: Achieving Continuous Performance Improvement

At the end of the day, what matters most to your organization's future is that you improve engagement/retention, increase revenue, control your costs, and maximize your overall organizational performance. In other words, you achieve continuous performance improvement.

Best practices may sound easy, but that's only in a perfect world. Our research shows many organizations aren't using the most optimal strategies for donor management, which means they fail to reach their highest performance levels.

iMIS 20 can help you reduce costs, maximize revenue, lower your risk, increase lifetime value, enhance engagement and improve organizational performance. Let's now take a look at how we've proven this.

We Can Ensure Continuous Performance Improvement

To achieve continuous performance improvement, several elements are absolutely vital:

- A clear strategy with long-range resource investment planning approved by the board that's currently being implemented

- Consistent discipline in measuring results and performance that allows management to be proactive and avoid external demands and crisis management
- A nimble management system for configuration and change management to accelerate donor engagement
- Departmental processes that encourage growth
- All-in-one donor management systems that ease staff and/or volunteer burden and increase donor convenience
- Top-rated, on-going staff training that increases operational productivity
- A single system with real-time data reporting/analysis for more informed decision making
- Accurate donor intelligence that allows for personalization and extends lifetime value

Our expert staff of Performance Improvement Specialists for fundraising organizations and our consultants will work with you to align your organization with all of the above. iMIS 20 was designed to address all of these elements once a client is positioned correctly to take advantage of them.

We Can Reduce Your Costs

Over a three-year period, the iMIS 20 EMS will cost about five times less than a traditional system. Sound unbelievable? It's true. And, it's because most organizations look at the initial cost of a new system and don't consider the related costs for ongoing customization programming, integration with new technologies, integration between disparate systems, related staff/management costs to maintain the system, and other "hidden costs."

Here's an example: The chart below compares the costs of an iMIS 20 EMS system that can address all of the "system costs"— right out-of-the-box — and what that same solution would cost if using a traditional model. It's a 5X difference — what organization can afford to pay 5 times more than it planned to and be locked into this for 5 to 7 years or more?

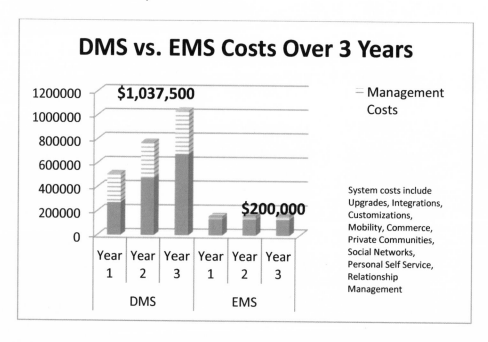

We Can Deliver Strong ROI

It's entirely possible to increase revenue from strong donor engagement/retention while at the same time decreasing costs as a result of smart, well-informed decisions. You can do this if you have a modern system like the iMIS 20 EMS, along with the right programs, tools and services from ASI, your trusted advisor.

The graph below shows what you can achieve over a seven-year period with iMIS 20; nearly flat costs and fast-rising revenues. Notice how the revenue line grows strong while the cost line barely increases. This is how the iMIS 20 EMS delivers a strong return on your system investment that can then be reinvested in your organization.

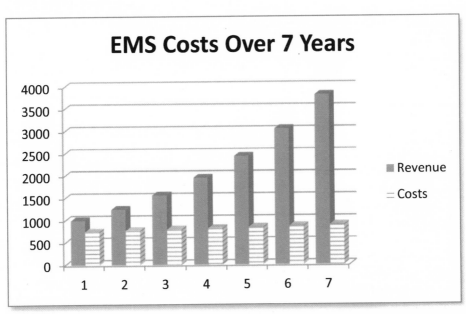

Source: Internal ASI research/client feedback.

We Exceed Expectations: Client Success Stories

At this stage, we'd like to share a few success stories of clients who have followed the best practices we've outlined and have achieved some of the goals we know you want to achieve. To read about more client success please visit www.advsol.com/success.

The Guide Dog Foundation for the Blind

The Guide Dog Foundation for the Blind provides guide dogs and training – free of charge – to people who are blind, visually impaired, or have other special needs. America's VetDogs was founded by the Guide Dog Foundation as the canine corps to serve the needs of disabled veterans and active duty personnel.

> *"We have had to take a look at reducing our staff costs and have done things to try and reduce staff without reducing services. iMIS helps us be more productive by integrating all of the information across all platforms. Revenue is rising; we have revenue coming from new sources."*

Challenge

Due to changes in the economy, the organizations were forced to reduce staff costs. Their challenge was to make these cuts without reducing the services they provided or affecting the quality of the programs. They also needed to look at creative ways to raise additional funds.

Solution

With iMIS, the Guide Dog Foundation and America's VetDogs were able to maintain all of their constituent data in one place -- tracking purchases as well as the number of gifts received, the amounts, and the specific appeals that generated them. They have used iMIS in multiple ways across all departments to increase productivity -- from enhancing volunteer management to generating general ledger and accounts receivable batches.

Results

Revenue is up and they are raising funds from new sources. The Guide Dog Foundation and America's VetDogs are seeing efficiency gains and are increasing program service success. The volunteer program is really growing and they're seeing all the different ways volunteers are able to work with them and help their programs. They are spreading their message around the world and showing what a difference people can make in each other's lives.

Rethink Mental Illness

Rethink Mental Illness is the operating name of the National Schizophrenia Fellowship. Rethink Mental Illness changes attitudes and policy by providing expert, accredited advice, services and information to the millions who are affected by mental health problems. The organization directly supports nearly 60,000 people each year across England; it has more than 200 mental health services and 150 support groups covering psychological therapies, crisis and recovery houses, peer support groups and housing services.

> *"The reduction in administration and overhead costs is significant. We used to spend ages collating all sorts of information manually for our reports but now iMIS is the portal for everything Rethink does. Many routine reports are generated automatically through iMIS and our Board members are astonished at the detail and accuracy of the new analysis."*

The Challenge

Rethink Mental Illness needed to find a new system that could manage multiple constituent types and revenue sources. Fundraising is an element of the Charity's £50m income; most income is received from grants and service contracts from health authorities/local governments to enable the Charity to provide high-quality services. A small but important part of its revenue is generated from around 3,000 members who pay monthly contributions. The Charity was using multiple systems to manage its various programs; these data silos made multi-channel marketing impossible and reporting a time-consuming nightmare.

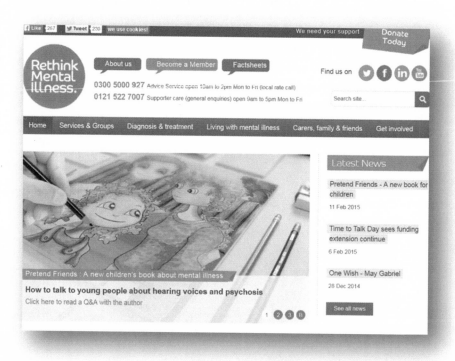

The Solution

Rethink Mental Illness selected iMIS because it provides one centralized solution for fundraising, membership and service activity management. The organization has 1,400 live iMIS users in 200 locations across the UK and can now manage most of its critical business data in a single database. This allows it to further segment its data for more personalized, targeted fundraising and marketing campaigns. Staff can access comprehensive, constituent intelligence that helps them make smarter business decisions. And, Rethink Mental Illness is also using iMIS to manage its Member and Donor websites to increase engagement with supporters.

The Results

With iMIS, Rethink Mental Illness was able to reduce administrative and overhead costs while also boosting productivity. It consolidated and streamlined its database from 300,000 contacts to 180,000 by removing duplicates and other bad data, thereby cutting expenses wasted on marketing to obsolete contacts. Manual reporting is now a thing of the past; most reporting is automatic and the organization has impressed its Board with invaluable, in-depth reporting.

Chalice

Chalice is a ministry of the Catholic community that creates and nurtures relationships of life and love with more than 45,000 children in the developing world. Chalice has 55 sponsor sites in 15 different countries and receives support from donations as well as from those who sponsor an individual child through a monthly recurring contribution.

> *"With iMIS efficiencies, Chalice has been able to improve our fundraising, enlarge our service area, increase transparency with real-time reporting, and extend staff time devoted to meeting the needs of our generous sponsors and the deserving children we are committed to help."*

The Challenge

The organization had been using a proprietary program that didn't have the flexibility and functionality to meet its growing needs. Chalice needed to manage multiple relationships -- with and among the children, sponsors, donors, and organization itself. For years, data on each child was being entered at the sponsor site and then re-entered into the Chalice system.

The organization wanted to better understand what was going on with the children it was monitoring, manage the correspondence/photos regularly sent from each child to sponsors, and implement better tools to measure organizational performance.

The Solution

After implementing iMIS, sponsor sites were provided remote access to enter information directly into the system, thereby relieving data entry burdens. The organization was able to enhance constituent communications, improve tracking to ensure sponsor wishes were being honored, and gain greater visibility into the particular needs of the children.

Within iMIS, Chalice was able to closely monitor its fundraising and access the data in real-time, which aided in reporting to various agencies and constituents -- and improved decision making.

The Results

Chalice now has the real-time data it needs to help fulfill its important mission. iMIS saves 4-5 staff days per month, thereby freeing employees to focus more attention on fostering a deeper relationship between sponsors and children. Chalice has been achieving 7% annual growth over the past 5 years without hiring additional data entry staff. Retention rates are up to 95%, and the organization has received top grades for transparency and trustworthiness due in part to iMIS' tracking and reporting capabilities. Chalice has even been able to expand its relief efforts to include Haiti.

The Cerebral Palsy League (CPL) of Queensland

The Cerebral Palsy League (CPL) of Queensland is a not-for-profit organization that provides vital support to more than 8,000 children and adults with cerebral palsy and physical disabilities. CPL provides services every day, at every stage of their clients' lives and has been doing so for over 65 years in thousands of homes, schools, communities and workplaces across Queensland and Northern NSW. CPL's total constituency tops 35,000, donors, volunteers and other supporters.

> *"Thanks to iMIS we now have a complete 360 degree view of our constituents and this allows us to more effectively manage our donors and grow our fundraising programs."*

The Challenge

CPL is the largest non-government disability services provider for people with a physical disability in Queensland but still needs to raise funds for equipment, services and programs. It was vital that the organization had a software solution it could rely on that was both comprehensive and easy to use. It was also important to work with a company that had a solid track record of success in the not-for-profit sector.

The Solution

With iMIS, CPL was able to manage fundraising, special events, lottery ticket sales and web functionality from a single, upgradeable software solution. They were able to adapt iMIS functionality to their core business, streamline their processes, monitor their database and launch communication strategies to keep constituents better informed while reducing manual tasks for staff.

The Results

After implementing iMIS on time and under budget, the Cerebral Palsy League quickly began to see a return on its investment. A combination of more efficient data processing, an integrated automatic dialing solution and a single database of constituent information allow CPL to deliver improved fundraising programs with a software system that has more control and is easier to use.

Chapter 6 — Next Steps: Success Partnership Program (SPP)

The Success Partnership Program (SPP) is designed to assist senior-level executives of not-for-profits organizations get the most out of their technology investments. We help you plan and execute the alignment of your operations with strategy. Our objective is to partner with you as your trusted advisor to permanently enable continuous performance improvement within your organization.

> ***Visit www.advsol.com/sppvideo to see a message from Bob Alves about the value of the SPP.***

The first step is our 25-point complimentary, no-risk Fundraising Success Assessment™ (see Chapter 2 — Assessing Your Current Situation). We compare your operations to industry best practices and prepare a report that is yours to keep. And based on our findings we determine whether your organization is a good fit for this program.

If you continue with the program, we next conduct a hands-on workshop to review the assessment with you and key staff. Many clients move from there to a smooth and efficient *"Performance Improvement Preview"* to help them experience the potential of working with us toward continuous performance improvement.

The SPP is designed to help you proactively identify your critical needs quickly, prepare a technology investment plan you can communicate to your Board with confidence that it will align with your organizational strategy, and – if you desire – ensure that anyone you work with in the future can accurately address your issues. This approach ultimately saves you time, reduces costs, and significantly lowers your risk of investing in the wrong technology assets and repeating the mistakes you may have made in the past.

> ***To learn more about how the Success Partnership Program (SPP) works see the Addendum.***

About the Authors

Bob Alves
Chairman and CEO
Advanced Solutions
International (ASI)

Don Robertson
President and CTO
Advanced Solutions
International (ASI)

Bob Alves is not your average corporate leader. He is unlike the many CEOs who remain faceless atop an organization chart, far removed from the company's everyday operations. An ASI Founding Partner more than 20 years ago, Bob is involved to this day in every critical aspect of the company – its present and the planning and design of its future.

After receiving his Bachelor of Business Administration degree from George Washington University, Bob went to work in the non-profit industry. He began as founder and President of DISC in 1982, a non-profit technology consulting company. DISC was acquired by software developer Smith Abbott in 1987, where Bob served as Vice President of Corporate Development.

Bob has always had a strong entrepreneurial spirit. After wrestling with the general lack of proper client service and absence of uniform products for the non-profit technology marketplace, he was inspired to found ASI in 1991. Driven by the mission of "keeping clients for life," ASI developed iMIS – advanced, easily upgradeable, and backed by a world-class, global network of trained client support staff.

Don Robertson is a widely known architect for positive change in the non-profit software industry, deftly building the future, not with concrete or steel, but with the dynamic processes of software. Don's vision has impacted more than 4,000 non-profits around the world.

Before helping to found ASI in 1991, Don honed his craft with Texas Instruments, American Standard and non-profit software developer Smith Abbott. While providing software consulting services at Smith Abbott, Don was struck by the lack of reliable, flexible and scalable software solutions for non-profit organizations.

Determined to remedy the situation, Don dedicated himself to the idea of pioneering software that could effectively manage an organization's constituency, communications and resources. iMIS became that solution. Today, it remains the flagship product of the award-winning company he helped create.

As President and Chief Technology Officer (CTO) of ASI, Don works hard every day to advance the company's philosophy through its technology. Don has a deep affection for the non-profit industry, is an ardent supporter of the community and an active participant within it.

About ASI

Advanced Solutions International (ASI) is a recognized global, industry thought leader that focuses on helping not-for-profits and not-for-profits increase operational and financial performance through the use of best practices, proven solutions, and ongoing client advisement.

We are the provider of iMIS 20, an Engagement Management System (EMS)™ that enables organizations to engage donors, donors, and other constituents anytime, anywhere, from any device.

We also have a global network of nearly 100 partners to provide you with a full range of services to implement and support your iMIS system.

Locations

USA
901 N. Pitt St., Suite 200
Alexandria, VA 22314
1-800-727-8682

Canada
251 Consumers Rd., Suite 1404
Toronto, ON Canada M2J 4R3
1-800-727-8682

Europe
2 Station Court, Imperial Wharf
London SW6 2PY
+44(0)20 3267 0067

Asia-Pacific
Level 22, 459 Collins Street
Melbourne VIC 3000
+61 3 9869 7500

Connect with Us

 www.advsol.com   @advsol   advanced-solutions-international-inc.

Addendum

The Success Partnership Program (SPP)

Overview

ASI's Success Partnership Program (SPP) is a no-risk way to assess, document, and test your specific needs in a real-world environment —using your own data and processes — and to learn exactly how the iMIS 20 Engagement Management System (EMS)™ can help before you decide to invest.

It's more than just a test drive: we work in partnership with you to understand your goals/objectives and then help you find the best methods to continuous performance improvement.

For a nominal engagement fee (which can be applied to your new iMIS system), you'll come away with a highly personalized report that documents everything you need from your next system in order to improve your overall results. You can then use this report to make an informed decision about iMIS — or any other potential system.

Benefits

No Risk

The SPP allows you to validate what you need from a new system before investing. At the end of the engagement, the SPP fee will be applied in full to your new iMIS system.

If you decide iMIS is not for you, you walk away with a finely tuned review report that is a far better predictor of your success than an RFP. No risk, no hassle, no downside.

More Effective

A system chosen through an RFP process rarely meets expectations because the process typically documents and then replicates current inefficiencies. We partner with you to understand your vital business processes, identify any possible gaps, and recommend the best and most modern methods to improve your overall results. We ask the tough questions and help you find the right answers by testing in a real-time, real-world environment.

Faster

In less than 90 days you can complete the program and know precisely what your organization requires and how iMIS can meet those challenges. No long, expensive, frustrating RFP process — and no guesswork.

Lower Cost

RFPs often require extensive staff time to brief multiple vendors over and over and lead to increased staff burden and expenses. The SPP minimizes internal costs, maximizes productivity, and gives a better return on your investment.

Performance Improvement Process

1. Operational Assessment

We compare your operations to industry best practices and prepare a report that is yours to keep.

2. Requirements Gathering

We review your current system, discuss desired functionality with your team, and document your requirements.

3. Performance Improvement Preview

We provide a preview of the iMIS 20 Engagement Management System (EMS) using your data and critical processes.

4. Key Performance Indicator Review

We help you to identify Key Performance Indicators (KPIs) relevant to your organization.

5. Performance Improvement Plan

We provide a final Performance Improvement Plan that documents your specific processes, critical needs, desired functionality, important KPIs, and more.

2015 Global Fundraising Performance Report

Executive Summary

ASI is proud to present our first annual Global Benchmark Report on Fundraising Performance, which explores the results, challenges, and goals of not-for-profits across North America, Europe, and Asia-Pacific. The survey was conducted in the summer/fall of 2014 and includes responses from 326 fundraising executives.

Key Findings

Fundraising organizations appear to be far more concerned with acquiring new donors than with retaining their existing base. It's vital to actively engage donors to maximize their lifetime value, but it appears that not-for-profits don't have the tools to do this and/or to measure the results. A startling number (30%) of executives surveyed don't even know their overall retention rate.

More than one-third (37%) of all executives disclose that their donor base is stagnant or declining. Yet improving donor retention is not an important objective. Despite the number of tools available on the market today, 24% of the surveyed executives reported that they do not know their donor engagement rates. On the bright side, they do recognize that they need real-time visibility into donor data to make informed decisions and are making this a priority.

Greatest Challenges

Survey participants identified several challenges they're currently facing and their top two were nearly tied. A lack of mobile and online fundraising capabilities was definitely a concern, as was their inability to adequately measure the engagement levels of their donors. These concerns were followed by a lack of integration between s donor management systems (DMS) and their websites. All of these concerns are obviously interrelated.

Top Goals

Not surprisingly, fundraising executives are focused on increasing donations, acquiring new contributors, and expanding the engagement levels of their existing bases. While increasing donor retention is also a consideration, it's not at the top of the list and that could be a problem. With the rising cost of new acquisitions, these organizations may wish to focus more on keeping their existing donor bases and increasing overall lifetime values.

Highest Priorities

Fundraising executives have two primary priorities at this time: 1) accessing/analyzing better intelligence on their donors and 2) taking advantage of the growing online and mobile fundraising opportunities available to them. However, there is a disconnect between their stated goals and highest priorities. To increase donations and engagement as well as improve donor intelligence and online capabilities, executives must first look at their donor management systems (and the systems' ability to integrate with their websites) to ensure they have the infrastructures to support their efforts.

Additional Findings

The survey provided interesting insight in several issue areas:

Engagement/Retention

Fundraising executives are heavily focused on attracting new donors vs. keeping those they've already paid dearly to acquire. They may be missing the boat by not paying more attention to programs and support systems that can help them retain more of their current bases — and do so more economically. The lack of emphasis on retention is reflected in the finding that one-third (30%) of all respondents don't even know their overall retention rate. And, the fact that 45% have declining or stagnant retention rates seems to indicate that they have not yet found the optimal methods to address the issue.

The good news is that more than half of all respondents (51%) have a greater than 50% retention rate and 11% have even achieved a 90%+ rate. However, 5% report a 90%+ turnover rate. That's a lot of work for such a small return — these not-for-profits must find ways to increase their retention rates in order to thrive.

Executives seem to have a better grasp on engagement, as 47% reported that it's up, while 29% indicated engagement rates are unchanged or declining. And, a heartening 83% claim they have a strategic initiative or tactical plan to improve donor engagement rates. Yet nearly a quarter of all survey participants report that they're unable to measure engagement. This underscores the urgent need to improve reporting capabilities.

Reporting

The need to improve reporting and donor intelligence seems to stem from a lack of key data points that executives must have to make important decisions and successfully guide their organizations into the future. 16% don't know what percentage of contributions were made online or through a mobile device and, as already reported, 24% can't currently measure engagement. Without this information, many executives are essentially "flying blind" without the benefit of intelligence that would help them make better business decisions.

Mobile/Social

40% of all survey participants report they offer no mobile options to their donors. Yet nearly another one-third (29%) indicate that they generated up to half of all their donations online. There is tremendous potential for not-for-profits here — and a huge missed opportunity if they choose to ignore mobile and online fundraising options. Executives seem to have lessened their interest a bit in social media but report that Facebook (followed closely by Twitter) is considered the most effective social media tool for achieving their fundraising goals.

Technology

Updating the website is a priority but it falls well below the need to improve reporting and online/ mobile options. More than one-third (35%) of respondents report they haven't redesigned their website in more than 3 years.

Three-quarters of all survey participants disclose that donor data and their websites are not integrated; 78% use disparate donor management systems and website content management systems (CMS), thereby making dynamic, personalized content more time-consuming and difficult to produce. And, while boosting donations and improving reporting are top concerns, data silos and the lack of web/data integration is not regarded as a big issue for executives. Yet these very data silos are likely making donor engagement more cumbersome and preventing organizations from maximizing lifetime value.